EARTH'S HISTORY THROUGH ROCKS

MOVING ICE

HOW THE GREAT LAKES FORMED

THERESA EMMINIZER

PowerKiDS press.
New York

Published in 2020 by The Rosen Publishing Group, Inc.
29 East 21st Street, New York, NY 10010

First Edition

Editor: Sarah Machajewski
Book Design: Tanya Dellaccio

Photo Credits: Cover Posnov/Moment Open/Getty Images; p. 5 Weredragon/Shutterstock.com; p. 7 (top) John Sidorowicz/Shutterstock.com; p. 7 (bottom) LesPalenik/Shutterstock.com; p. 9 https://upload.wikimedia.org/wikipedia/commons/e/ef/Sea_Ice_off_Baffin_Island.jpg; p. 11 (top) SF photo/Shutterstock.com; p. 11 (bottom) Alex Dumitrescu/Shutterstock.com; p. 13 John McCormick/Shutterstock.com; p. 14 Elena Elisseeva/Shutterstock.com; p. 15 UniversalImagesGroup/Universal Images Group/Getty Images; p. 17 (top left) DeymosHR/Shutterstock.com; p. 17 (top right) Gilberto Mesquita/Shutterstock.com; p. 17 (bottom) Wally Stemberger/Shutterstock.com; p. 19 Print Collector/Hulton Archive/Getty Images; p. 21 (top) https://commons.wikimedia.org/wiki/Category:Le_Griffon_(ship,_1679)#/media/File:Image_taken_from_page_44_of_%27Annals_of_Fort_Mackinac%27_(11279194954).jpg; p. 21 (bottom) https://upload.wikimedia.org/wikipedia/commons/c/c5/Cavelier_de_la_salle.jpg; p. 23 (top) Graham Taylor Photography/Shutterstock.com; p. 23 (bottom) StonePhotos/Shutterstock.com; p. 25 (top) Karen Bell/Shutterstock.com; p. 25 (bottom) Erni/Shutterstock.com; p. 27 (top) Basotxerri/Shutterstock.com; p. 27 (bottom) Scott Olsen/Getty Images News/Getty Images; p. 29 Chicago Tribune/Tribune News Service/Getty Images; p. 30 Helen Filatova/Shutterstock.com.

Cataloging-in-Publication Data

Names: Emminizer, Theresa.
Title: Moving ice: how the Great Lakes formed / Theresa Emminizer.
Description: New York : PowerKids Press, 2020. | Series: Earth's history through rocks | Includes glossary and index.
Identifiers: ISBN 9781725301566 (pbk.) | ISBN 9781725301580 (library bound) | ISBN 9781725301573 (6pack)
Subjects: LCSH: Glacial lakes–Great Lakes (North America) | Glacial epoch–Great Lakes (North America) | Geology–Great Lakes (North America)–Juvenile literature. | Great Lakes (North America)–Juvenile literature.
Classification: LCC F551.E46 2020 | DDC 551.31'50977–dc23

Manufactured in the United States of America

CPSIA Compliance Information: Batch #CSPK19. For Further Information contact Rosen Publishing, New York, New York at 1-800-237-9932.

CONTENTS

WHAT ARE THE GREAT LAKES? 4
BEGINNING WITH BEDROCK 6
GLACIERS ON THE MOVE 8
THE EARLY LAKES 10
READING THE ROCKS 12
LAKE STATS 14
THE WATERS' FLOW 16
THE HISTORY OF THE GREAT LAKES 18
THE MYSTERY OF *LE GRIFFON* 20
A MAINSPRING OF ECONOMY 22
AN ECOLOGICAL TREASURE 24
THREATS TO ADDRESS 26
CONSERVATION EFFORTS 28
GIFTS FROM THE PAST 30
GLOSSARY 31
INDEX 32
WEBSITES 32

WHAT ARE THE GREAT LAKES?

The Great Lakes and their connecting waterways make up the largest surface freshwater system on Earth. They're sometimes called the Laurentian Great Lakes. The five lakes in this system are Lake Superior, Lake Michigan, Lake Huron, Lake Erie, and Lake Ontario. The Saint Marys, Saint Clair, Detroit, and Niagara rivers, with other smaller waterways, connect them.

The Great Lakes are mighty both in size and importance. They hold about 6 quadrillion gallons (22.7 quadrillion L) of water. Their combined surface spans over 94,000 square miles (244,000 sq. km). The lakes support thousands of plant and animal species, as well as the economy of the surrounding states and regions.

The Great Lakes are some of North America's most treasured geological features. How exactly did these amazing lakes form? The story begins hundreds of millions of years ago.

There's enough water in the Great Lakes to cover the continental United States in nearly 10 feet (3 m) of water!

READING THE ROCKS

THE GREAT LAKES ARE HOME TO THE BIGGEST SUPPLY OF FRESHWATER IN THE WORLD. THEY HOLD ABOUT 90 PERCENT OF THE SURFACE FRESHWATER IN THE UNITED STATES AND ABOUT ONE-FIFTH OF THE TOTAL SURFACE FRESHWATER IN THE WORLD!

BEGINNING WITH BEDROCK

The rocks of the Great Lakes formed much earlier than the lakes themselves. These rocks are made of many layers. The bottom layer is bedrock—the hard, solid rock that lies underneath loose deposits of soil. The bedrock in the Great Lakes **basin** formed over two time periods. The deepest layer is made of **metamorphosed** igneous and sedimentary rocks from the Precambrian period. These rocks formed between 36 billion and 1 billion years ago.

The Precambrian bedrock gradually wore away due to erosion. Later, seas covered the Great Lakes basin, depositing sediments on top of the eroded Precambrian bedrock. The second layer of bedrock, called the Phanerozoic bedrock, includes sedimentary rocks such as shale and limestone.

The Precambrian period is the earliest geologic age. It occurred 4.5 billion to 542 million years ago. The Precambrian rocks pictured here make up the Canadian Shield, a mass of rock in eastern Canada and the northeastern United States.

GLACIERS ON THE MOVE

About 500,000 years ago, during a period called the Pleistocene Epoch, temperatures in North America dropped. The cold temperatures and increased **precipitation** caused **glaciation**. Glacial snow and ice built up on the land over thousands of years. The heavy glacial ice pressed the earth down, causing it to sink in certain places. Deep, wide **depressions** formed.

Later, as temperatures began to warm, the ice retreated. The glacier carved out new landforms as it slid slowly across the land. This glacial movement is what created the Great Lakes about 14,000 years ago.

As the glacier slid, it picked up rocks and chunks of earth, carried them away, and deposited them elsewhere. This created a layer of loose sediment.

THE LAURENTIDE ICE SHEET

The Great Lakes are in a part of North America that was once entirely covered with ice. The Laurentide Ice Sheet covered more than 5 million square miles (13 million sq. km) and was more than 8,000 feet (2,438 m) thick. The last piece of the Laurentide Ice Sheet is now in the Canadian Arctic. Scientists study the rocks around what remains of the ice sheet to see how it has grown and shrunk over millions of years.

Today, glaciers cover 10 percent of the total land area in the world. During the last ice age, ice covered almost 32 percent of Earth's land.

READING THE ROCKS

THE LAST GLACIATION TO TAKE PLACE IN NORTH AMERICA IS CALLED THE WISCONSIN GLACIAL STAGE. DURING THIS TIME, MANY NEW LANDFORMS WERE CREATED IN THE REGION THAT IS NOW WISCONSIN.

THE EARLY LAKES

As the glacier retreated, it melted, filling in the deep depressions it left behind. These depressions became the early forms of what would become the Great Lakes.

The Great Lakes didn't always look like they do today. During their early days, the lakes and rivers changed in size and shape as new drainage systems were carved out by the moving glacier. For example, Lake Chicago and Lake Maumee, the **predecessors** of Lakes Michigan and Erie, once drained southward into the Mississippi River. It wasn't until later that the lakes began to drain east into the Saint Lawrence River and out into the Atlantic Ocean. At one time, the high water between Lakes Huron and Michigan formed one large lake called Lake Algonquin. Today, Lake Algonquin no longer exists.

HOW GLACIERS FORM

There are two main types of glaciers: alpine glaciers and ice sheets. The glacier that formed the Great Lakes was an ice sheet. A glacier is formed when snow **accumulates** each year and doesn't completely melt. Over time, the snow becomes tightly packed. In time, this packed snow grows thicker and fuses into solid ice. The weight of the glacier melts the snow at the bottom and the heavy mass begins to move.

There are about 35,000 islands throughout the Great Lakes. These were created by uneven glacial activity. Manitoulin in Lake Huron is the largest lake island on Earth. It's 1,068 square miles (2,766 sq. km).

READING THE ROCKS

GLACIERS MOVE VERY SLOWLY. USUALLY, THEY'RE ONLY ABLE TO TRAVEL AN INCH (2.5 CM) OR SO A DAY. HOWEVER, THEIR HEAVY WEIGHT MAKES THEM VERY POWERFUL. GLACIERS CARVE AND CARRY HUGE AMOUNTS OF ROCKS, SOIL, AND CLAY.

READING THE ROCKS

Geology is the scientific study of Earth's physical structure and history. How have geologists been able to determine all the information we now know about the Great Lakes? The history is recorded in the rocks. By studying the rock deposits of the Great Lakes, geologists have learned more about how and when they formed.

The movement of glaciers scraped away some of the Phanerozoic bedrock of the Great Lakes, which revealed the presence of the Precambrian bedrock. The glacial movement also left behind the loose sediment that now covers the bedrock.

The rock layers are more visible in some areas of the Great Lakes than in others. For example, the sedimentary bedrock is thicker in Michigan, and the Precambrian bedrock is more visible to the north.

The rocks shown here are located at the Lake Superior Pictured Rocks National Lakeshore in Michigan. Visitors can hike, camp, and ski there.

DATING ROCKS

How are geologists able to determine when rocks formed? They use **radiometric** dating! Tiny **radioactive** elements are present in all rocks. Over time, these elements break down into atoms. Because these elements break down at a fixed rate over time, geologists can measure how much they've broken down to determine a rock's age. The starting point for a radiometric measurement is when the rock formed.

LAKE STATS

Lake Superior is the largest and deepest Great Lake. Its surface area is 31,700 square miles (82,102.6 sq. km), with an average depth of 489 feet (149 m). Scientifically, Lakes Huron and Michigan are actually one body of water. The Straits of Mackinac connect the two bodies of water. The straits keep the water level between Lakes Michigan and Huron almost equal. Lake Michigan is the only Great Lake that's entirely within the United States.

Lake Erie is the shallowest of the lakes at 62 feet (19 m) deep on average. Lake Ontario is the smallest by surface area, covering 7,340 square miles (19,010.5 sq. km).

Based on surface area, Lake Superior is the second largest lake in the world.

LAKE SUPERIOR
LAKE HURON
LAKE ONTARIO
LAKE MICHIGAN
LAKE ERIE

THE WATERS' FLOW

The water in the Great Lakes flows roughly eastward from Lake Superior. It moves through the lakes into the Saint Lawrence River and pours into the Atlantic Ocean. The Great Lakes drain from Superior to Michigan and Huron to Erie to Ontario. Except for Lakes Michigan and Huron, the altitude, or height above sea level, of the lakes decreases from west to east in a downward slope. This causes water to flow faster as it moves into these lakes. Lakes Michigan and Huron are at about the same altitude.

The water from Lake Erie feeds into the Niagara River and then over the waterfalls that make up Niagara Falls before reaching Lake Ontario. Lake Ontario flows into the Saint Lawrence River at a rate of 242,000 cubic feet (6,852.7 cubic m) per second.

READING THE ROCKS

PRECIPITATION IS THE MAIN SOURCE OF WATER IN THE GREAT LAKES. MUCH PRECIPITATION IS LOST TO **EVAPORATION**. HOWEVER, WATER IS ALSO ADDED IN THE FORM OF RUNOFF, WHICH IS WATER THAT COLLECTS ON THE GROUND AND RUNS INTO THE LAKES.

Although the waterfalls of Niagara aren't the tallest in the world, they have the largest volume of water traveling through them. About 3,160 tons (2,866.7 mt) of water flow over Niagara Falls every second.

THE NIAGARA ESCARPMENT

The Niagara Escarpment is a steep cliff that runs in an arc from New York up through Canada and down to Illinois. Originally a seabed, it began to take shape over 450 million years ago. As the bodies of dead sea creatures mixed with mud and sand, they slowly compressed into rock. Over the millions of years that followed, the sea dried up and erosion changed the landscape, creating the cliffs we see today.

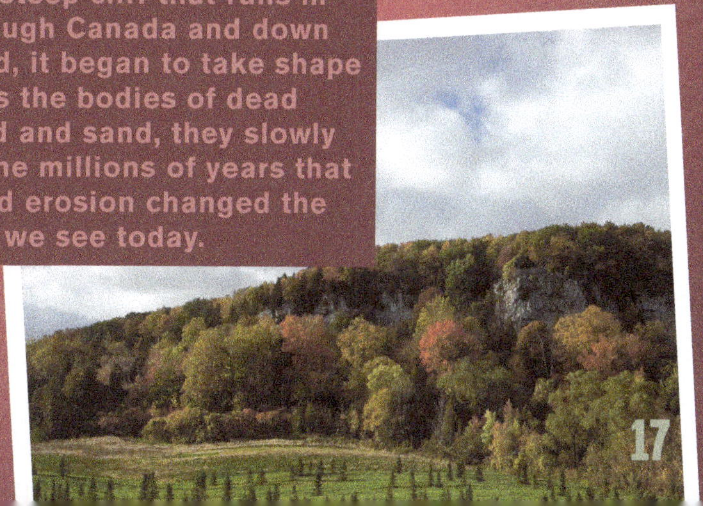

THE HISTORY OF THE GREAT LAKES

Native Americans were the first people to live in the Great Lakes basin. The Chippewa, Fox, Huron, Iroquois, Ottawa, Potawatomi, and Sioux peoples were among the many that called the Great Lakes region home. During the 1600s, French explorers began to visit the region. They began a fur trade with the native peoples of the Great Lakes.

The modern-day names of the Great Lakes are based on their original native names or on the French names for the tribes that inhabited the region. For example, in the Iroquois language, the name "Ontario" comes from a term that means "great lake" or "beautiful lake." "Michigan" comes from a Chippewa word meaning "large lake." The French referred to the Wyandot people who lived near Lake Huron as the Huron, so the lake received that name.

The native peoples of the Great Lakes often traded beaver pelts, or skins, to European explorers in exchange for guns and tools.

THE MYSTERY OF *LE GRIFFON*

The first full-size European ship to sail the upper Great Lakes was a French vessel called *Le Griffon*. It was launched in 1679 by explorer René-Robert Cavelier de La Salle, who hoped to expand the fur trade with the Native American peoples living on the Great Lakes.

On August 7, 1679, *Le Griffon* set sail on Lake Erie with a crew of 32 men. The voyage of *Le Griffon* took it across Lake Erie, Lake Huron, and Lake Michigan—waters that until then had only been traveled by canoe. La Salle came ashore on September 18, 1679. He sent the ship, manned by six crewmen, on its return voyage to the Niagara region without him. The ship, along with its crew and load of furs, vanished. The search for the lost ship still continues today.

Le Griffon has been nicknamed "the Ghost Ship of the Great Lakes."

RENÉ-ROBERT CAVELIER DE LA SALLE

A MAINSPRING OF ECONOMY

Le Griffon was first of many commercial ventures on the Great Lakes. From the 1600s onward, the region quickly grew as a center for trade. Since then, a multitude of industries (including shipping, manufacturing, agriculture, mining, energy services, and tourism) have **thrived** in the Great Lakes region. Gold, nickel, copper, iron ore, aluminum, silver, steel, and coal are a few of the minerals and metals found or produced in the area. Many of these materials are used in nearby auto and airplane manufacturing industries.

The surrounding states also export animal feed, vegetables, and chocolate to Canada. Today, more than half of the trade between the United States and Canada occurs across the lakes. Over 200 million tons (181.4 million mt) of cargo is shipped across the lakes each year.

The Great Lakes region supports over 51 million jobs. If the area were a country, it would have the third largest economy in the world!

HYDROELECTRIC POWER

The Great Lakes provide a huge source of renewable electricity in the form of hydroelectric power. Hydroelectric power, or hydropower, is the use of water to create electricity. In 1879, the first hydroelectric power plant was built at Niagara Falls. Hydroelectric power is the cheapest form of energy and produces about one-fifth of the world's electricity. Unfortunately, it can be damaging to natural resources and wildlife.

HYDROELECTRIC POWER PLANT, NIAGARA FALLS

AN ECOLOGICAL TREASURE

The ecosystem of the Great Lakes basin is large and **unique**. Because of their differences in size, depth, and temperature, the Great Lakes have become the **habitats** for a large variety of fish and wildlife species. The basin includes many different natural landscapes, such as rivers, forests, grasslands, and wetlands. Despite the rise of cities surrounding the Great Lakes, animals that traditionally made their homes in these habitats continue to do so today.

Lake trout, sturgeon, whitefish, and mussels make their home within the waters. Gray wolves, Canadian lynx, moose, river otters, beavers, and bald eagles inhabit the surrounding land. **Migratory** birds such as waterfowl rely on Great Lakes habitats as safe nesting areas. Observing the native wildlife can help scientists learn about the health of the whole ecosystem.

Mink, such as the one pictured here on the shore of Lake Ontario, feed on lake fish.

THREATS TO ADDRESS

Unfortunately, the Great Lakes and the creatures that live there are in danger. Many problems have upset the delicate balance of the Great Lakes ecosystems.

There are more than 180 nonnative species currently living in the Great Lakes region. Nonnative species, such as zebra mussels, compete for resources such as food with animals that are native to the area. **Climate change** also poses a major threat. The rising temperatures cause too much water to evaporate from the lakes, lowering water levels, endangering wetlands, and damaging water quality. Chemicals and toxins, such as industrial waste, sewage, and runoff from mining and cities, have polluted Great Lakes waters. It's estimated that 22 million pounds (10 million kg) of plastic waste enters the Great Lakes every year. These pollutants are harmful to both wildlife and people.

READING THE ROCKS

NONNATIVE SPECIES ARE OFTEN BROUGHT INTO THE GREAT LAKES BY SHIPS COMING FROM THE OCEAN. THESE SHIPS HAVE BALLAST TANKS, WHICH HOLD WATER. WHEN THE SHIPS DUMP THIS WATER, THEY CAN RELEASE NONNATIVE SPECIES INTO THE LAKES.

There are concerns over the levels of mercury in fish from the Great Lakes.

CONSERVATION EFFORTS

As a major freshwater resource in the United States and the world, the protection of the Great Lakes is of the greatest importance. To ensure that these national treasures remain healthy and productive, people and governments have been making conservation efforts to address the major dangers that threaten them.

State and federal government organizations such as the Environmental Protection Agency must keep a watchful eye on mining companies and manufacturing industries that put the lakes at risk. Community members can address the problems of litter and pollution by volunteering for beach cleanup days and making an effort to reduce the amount of trash they create. Conserving water and protecting wildlife habitats will be fundamental to the preservation of the Great Lakes.

Millions of people rely on the Great Lakes as a source of drinking water.

GIFTS FROM THE PAST

The exact age of the Great Lakes is still unknown. They were crafted in stone and carved out by glaciers over time, changing in character and form until about 14,000 years ago. Then, they began to take shape as the majestic geographic features we know today.

From the retreat of the Laurentide Ice Sheet to the arrival of humans, and from the formation of the Great Lakes basin to modern-day industrialization, these mighty lakes have experienced extraordinary change. In that time, they have proved to be an unmatched resource for freshwater, accounting for 20 percent of the freshwater in the entire world. By studying their amazing history, we've been able to learn more not just about the Great Lakes basin, but about the planet and the many forces that shape it.

GLOSSARY

accumulate: To gather or build up.

basin: An area that drains water from the surrounding land.

climate change: Change in Earth's weather caused by human activity.

depression: An area that dips lower than the surface surrounding it, forming a "bowl" where water can gather.

evaporation: The process of turning from liquid into gas.

glaciation: The process of being covered by glaciers or ice sheets.

habitat: The natural home for plants, animals, and other living things.

precipitation: Water that falls to the ground as hail, mist, rain, sleet, or snow.

predecessor: Something that comes before another.

metamorphosed: Changed in form.

migratory: Moving from one place to another.

radioactive: Giving off rays of light, heat, or energy.

radiometric: Relating to the measurement of radioactivity.

thrive: To grow successfully.

unique: Special or different from anything else.

INDEX

A

Algonquin, Lake, 10
Atlantic Ocean, 10, 16

C

Canada, 5, 6, 17, 22
Canadian Shield, 6
Chicago, Lake, 10
climate change, 26

D

Detroit River, 4

E

Environmental Protection Agency, 28
Erie, Lake, 4, 5, 10, 14, 15, 16, 20

G

glaciers, 8, 9, 10, 11, 12, 30

H

Huron, Lake, 4, 5, 10, 11, 14, 15, 16, 18, 20
hydropower, 23

P

Pennsylvania, 5
Phanerozoic bedrock, 6, 12
Pleistocene Epoch, 8
Precambrian period, 6, 12

R

radiometric dating, 13

S

Saint Clair River, 4
Saint Lawrence River, 10, 16
Saint Marys River, 4
Straits of Mackinac, 14
Superior, Lake, 4, 5, 12, 14, 15, 16

U

United States, 5, 6, 14, 22, 28

W

Wisconsin, 5, 9
Wisconsin glacial stage, 9

WEBSITES

Due to the changing nature of Internet links, PowerKids Press has developed an online list of websites related to the subject of this book. This site is updated regularly. Please use this link to access the list: www.powerkidslinks.com/EHTR/lakes